Houses Around the World

by Anne Giulieri

People live
all around the world.
Some people live
in very hot places.

Other people live
where it is cold
and there is lots of snow.

People can also live where there is lots of water.
It can be hard to live in these places.
People often have houses to fit the weather
where they live.

People who live in hot and dry places
build homes to keep them cool.
Some houses have thick mud walls.
These walls help to keep hot *air* out.
This keeps the inside of the house cool.

Other houses are built with sticks
or under the ground to keep people cool.

Houses made with sticks
give people *shade*
in very hot places.
It is always cooler
in the shade.

6

A house built under the ground helps
to stop hot air from coming inside.
This keeps the inside of the house cool.

People who live in cold places
build homes made for lots of snow.

8

A house made
for the snow sometimes
has a very *slanted roof.*
When the snow begins
to get too heavy,
it slides off the roof.
If the house had
a flat roof, heavy snow
could make the roof
fall in.

Long ago some people used blocks of *ice*
to make a place to stay.
A house made from blocks of ice is called an igloo.

Igloos helped people to keep warm and dry. People do not live in igloos very often now.

11

Some people live in places near the water.
Their houses need to be built
off the ground to keep them safe and dry.
Sometimes after a lot of rain,
the water in a river can go up.

A house built on *stilts* helps
to stop the water from coming inside.

Other people live on the water.

They live in houseboats or *floating houses*.

Their houses move up and down with the water.

As you can see, people live in all kinds of houses.
Which house would you like to live in?

Picture glossary

air

ice

slanted roof

floating houses

shade

stilts